A House by the River

By the same author

A House by the River

Diane Fahey

PUNCHER & WATTMANN

First published in 2016
Published by Puncher and Wattmann
PO Box 441
Glebe NSW 2037
http://www.puncherandwattmann.com
puncherandwattmann@bigpond.com

National Library of Australia
Cataloguing-in-Publication entry:

Fahey, Diane
A House by the River

ISBN 9781922186874
I. Title.
A821.3

Cover design by Matthew Holt

This project has been assisted by the
Australian Government through the Australia
Council, its arts funding and advisory body.   Australian Government

In memory of Patricia Brotheridge
18.06.1921 – 27.12.2008

Contents

I

II

III

IV

V

I

My Mother's Garden

The garden shines, soaked by night rain.
Over months we've unearthed ivy and dead shrubs,
bedded new camellias around those planted
long since by my father.
The smallest is lost to February heat,
others bear leaf-scars; but this grove will thrive.

Becoming, after lifelong resistance
a gardener, I sift soil for debris,
clearing stones and broken roots,
letting air into tamped earth.
Next, the embellishments – canna lilies,
impatiens, flax rising above white rocks;
by the front door, jade. We'll rest or work here,
breathe the sweet, salt-winnowed air.

Summer Rain

Rain falls in the middle of the night –
a statement, an unanswerable question.
Lightning flares for a sustained moment
in the rooms of the dreaming.
           Next day, the street flooded,
our dog's sequestered basket a damp nest
and every plant in the garden singing –
the enemy ivy, the brave and the fragile
it would strangle.
           Torrents rinsing away
the skin of dust on things, while stirring doubt.
A month's rain in a night; the pattern changing
until there's no pattern. Last winter dry
and this year's heat set to come in autumn –
when these refreshed leaves will fail; the molten
clamour of each dawn, a harbinger.

Night Sky

I stood with my mother in the garden.
No crescent moon to be seen, but the sky,
neither blue nor black, was present,
a silence opening the gaze.
Stars gave the usual unreadable clues
as to their provenance, their pathways.

If they, with the sky, composed a garment
you could wrap yourself in, a state
you could become, you would no longer,
perhaps, want life.
                         That page of brilliant dust
on almost-dry ink is, suffice to say,
a way of knowing this place,
and of knowing this place as infinitely
otherwise than we know it.

Their House

Bought for a song in 1972:
rusty walls and ceilings of pressed tin; no stumps;
a cramped main room. There was a sense of old chill.
My father refurbished it to survive him,
see out my mother's days – with, even then,
the conviction he should leave first.
Their home became snug yet never lost
that whiff of awkward exoticism:
among the town's oldest; in its first life
a boathouse, some say – a rumour I neither believe
nor disbelieve, would like to think is true.
These days I harbour dreams of seeing out
my own time on this piece of earth that has grown
weeds and flowers and trees with such abandon.

In the early years of the town of Barwon Heads, some landholders built boathouses
large enough to live in on their weekend and holiday visits.

Garden

A sound between breath and utterance
as breakers crumple to spindrift.
Above the heave of boughs, seagulls
surf the air, the swallows loop and feed.
We sit at ease by the myrtle willow,
its fronds astir; unmoved, the hibiscus
mauvely in bud, your burgundy roses.

Blackbirds, wattlebirds, stitch the trees
together: each soughing of wing feathers
a half-whisper from the unconscious.
Whenever the wind grows wilder
forest sounds without a forest; the speech of leaves
forced into one voice. Later, silence;
dusk unfolds like a hothouse flower.

In Late Autumn

These are the days when skies resume
The old – old sophistries of June –
A blue and gold mistake.

　　　　Emily Dickinson, 'Indian Summer'

A time to be still, let wonder hold sway.
So why are we working like this –
inside the gift of unseasonal light
without regarding it; our feet above
deep-cached cicadas as we unclench roots,
lop boughs, bring down canopies of creeper.

Soon the back garden, long derelict,
will be reclaimed. Our minds fix on hazards,
the next task; we dream of lavender and ferns,
sea thrift, azure irises.
The body gives its strength to this service,
to arrive, hours later, at a heartened fatigue.
Then it is time to stand and face this light,
to take its measure, be measured by it.

Winter

The first day, peerless – from ingenuous blue
no hint. But soon enough, the long rains
will arrive, wear out their welcome,
and bouts of hail thud on the iron roof
while gusts, whistling through cracks,
invade each nook, an icy presence:
the soul's gaze contracts, strength leaks from the marrow;
you become a thief of hope.

Then, the touchstones of garden and river,
silence and birdsong, new words on a raw page
must work their holding power – while this day
dreams its return in windfalls of light,
a spring sky travelled by swans and ibis,
winged seeds, the odd threadbare cloud.

The Onset

Back in the kingdom of rain.
The road to the pier's a black mirror,
the river, a torrent of shadows: beyond it,
trees, rooftops, smokily solid in the mist.
I bumble and stride over drenched sand,
my shoes sucked down, the wind
pitting my body against itself.

Within four walls, I think of farmers
in hope again, riverside dwellers'
rising fears – the rain, a haunting.
                              In these rooms
veiled with drowned light, we enter
a fallow stillness.
                    Through the runnelled pane
blood-red berries in pools, camellia and
rose leaves dripping; the whole garden drinking.

Fall

Even as I clear it, ivy claims more ground;
each downpour draws forth new suckers.
Ambushed, I meet hard earth,
my ankles a momentary sideways hinge:
a fall too swift to remember.
Red, indigo, chartreuse – the bruises bloom,
turn pastel-pale as an old fresco.

Day after day I lie curled inside time,
the mind-shadows cast by so much death
in strange abeyance. There's a rest from
onwardness, too: my body saturated with
its life so far, sealed against dissolution.
My feet are growing wings from the bruises;
storing strength for the next reach of the journey.

Sabrina

She can be seen touring the Grand Canal
on the prow of a Carpaccio gondola,
or near his Augustine in an airy
chamber furnished like a universe:
a companion of the work looking out, as now,
from bright, sober depths.
                    A reader of hearts and minds –
yet smell is her religion, the world
a scent map constantly updated.

Epicurean before weeds, dirtily
curious at tree trunks, she'll dawdle past
dogs rearing from leashes, but quakes at
storms that douse the walls,
                    set moonless skies on fire:
we hear her scratching at the kitchen door
to be safe again, and not alone.

Maltese Terriers are depicted in Vittore Carpaccio's *Miracle of the Cross at the Ponte di Rialto* and his *Saint Augustine in his Study.*

Walking the Dog

At the gate I break threads of daylight:
a web tilts, its curled leaf swathed in gnat wings,
petals from the climbing-rose.
                                    We go forth.
In the many pauses of our progress
I daydream under the heady swish of
tree tops or, ringed by swallows,
on the marram-tufted shore.

A day of earth scents, swells and lulls
of air – its touch a counterpoint to light's
sumptuous embrace. A sense of worlds
within and beyond this one, waiting to be known
while, as the wind draws in breath, we –
this ruby-tongued white dog and I – are held
with all living beings, in the balance.

The Myrtle Willow

I've read sadness and pique in Sabrina's eyes
along with breathtaking need-and-love.
Today I find knowledge of death in them, too.
Yes, all will end: the round of small, obsessive
pleasures; the solace of touch and propinquity –
there are many old ecstasies between us.

At six, middle-aged, she takes no commands,
each walk a wayward line through flowering streets,
the moonah woodlands: in her driven quest
suggestible to a fault, as I am.
As we rest by the willow, her gaze deepens,
becomes a mirror-pool of the unsaid.
Cool air stirs the lilacs whose scent she savours
with the merest twitch of her nose, her third eye.

Night Burial

Hours later than was promised, she's brought
wrapped in a towel, straight from the vet's freezer.
In the waiting room she'd stood stiffly,
unable to lie down, her molten eyes
signalling what I guessed, would soon be told.
We walk out to the garden grave by torchlight.
Camellias, a bunch of bluebells
rain down on three kilos of flesh and fur.

If, as we can't but hope, lost life becomes
a gifting presence, here's what she'd be.
A small white queen, walking or floating near
willow and plum tree, my father's wild rose bush –
equally at peace in cold wind or sunlight;
ranging freely; smelling only the flowers.

Spring

Cherry blossoms –
lights
of years past.

      Matsuo Bashō

It begins early: from midwinter on,
boughs ruched with blossoms that halt my walks,
not, (drawn by such frail abundance),
to lose myself in them, but to contemplate
worlds of light grown from darkness,
call up a spring haiku:
                        an inwardly flowering seed
poised in eternity's gold air.

Our camellias next, even the tree with split
branch yielding seven-day wonders;
this sleeper, bare for years, now
recklessly crimsoned.
                  And the geraniums?
A faithfulness without season,
giving and giving of their plain reds, pinks;
asking only a little sun, a little rain.

New Holland Honeyeaters

Seducers, pirates, acrobats –
tides of them sweep through the spring garden,
their feathers wind-tweaked as they balance
and reach, sipping from bloom after bloom
of monbretia, carnivalesque inside
each orange mask – one petal upright,
an eye each side; bird and flower conjoined.

*Give me a place to perch and I will drink
the world*, they seem to say, their voices pitched
between squeaky toy, whirring tin top;
the sound of their wings a shuffled card deck.
Now, nectar-fuelled gossip, bouts of
amorous chasey, the tending of young –
a swift transfer of sweetness, beak to beak.

Rainbow Lorikeets

Who said you could breeze in –
                                            a host of sunsets,
orange-and-gold, emblazoned on your breasts –
to fill the garden with the cut and thrust
of speech, making side-comments as you feast
and marking this peach tree on summer's map:
its lushness waning as stones drop like hail
while new sites start to glow, linked by
songlines, flight-lines, apricot- and plum-lines.

Underlids glint as I draw near.
Sated, you give your blessing:
with gentle sentience, Eden eyes look down.
Then you've other trees to flit through
with shrieks and clacks that celebrate being:
its powered beauty, its blissful fruitiness.

Feeding the Birds

They wait in the trees for her, morning and evening –
doves mostly, with speckled torque on neck,
and sparrows, lighter than air, sporting plumage
of moccha, latte-beige. The seeds fan out.
Our guest, an escaped bantam, dips as if
crossing waves in her body-boat of muscled snow:
even the small-brained have their sublime touches –
a lemon phosphorescence on cheeks, old gold
beak, red jelly dewlaps and coiffure.
Now the magpies fly in: doves, sparrows disperse.
Rogue sunflowers tower beside my mother
as she stands – her garden, brought back from wildness,
growing around her freshly,
holding her in its open embrace.

Garden Walk

A stand of ivory irises, gold-tongued,
cinerarias in royal velvets.
We pass my father's camellia tree,
its yield of coral cups the first since his death.
Long years. You call it 'the miracle tree'.
Nearby, this mandala bloom: splayed petals
frame the abounding heart, heart-red.

I think of these hopeful, circumspect days
as your harvest won from pain endured;
this garden, your own small share
of life's quest for beauty in survival.
At dusk, whether we listen or not,
bird songs will wreathe this old house in splendour.
Later, lotus-stars on a black pond.

II

Interior

Between rain bursts, light emanates like heat
from moonstone clouds. The word-filled screen
above my desk falls dark: I rest,
listening to poetry on the radio –
a gravitas wrought from uncertainty,
from night thoughts, cryptic or ragged,
and the gifts brought by unknown tides.

Amidst this scatter of typescripts, of scored
first drafts, chaos nurtures connection;
a chosen stillness wakens the inner eye.
The travel-poster sky above Salzburg,
the blue of my socks, and that clasping
the dolphin in the photo, elide with shifting
glimpses of a zenith, larkspur-blue.

3 a.m. Waking

After typing, and getting snacks,
and eyeing the slew of drafts on my bed
I slip back in, numbed by fatigue, my bones
feeling the drilled-out years of walking the line.
I read Dickinson's 'The last night that she lived',
Eavan Boland's 'I Remember'
and, by Mary Oliver, 'Wild Geese'.

Then I start this, bolstered high so the pen
won't falter, but sliding slowly under
the counterpane of poems
as words come fast.
                    The ink stops. I hear the birds.
Never give up: sing to mark your space,
establish your life's domain – the tone piquant,
a gold spoon tapping on crystal.

On Dreams

It needs a strong will, and patience,
to hold the dream inside the body
while the mind imprints itself with
                              icons of bright smoke
and a hand reaches for pen, paper.
Timed out, the dream's beyond reclaim,
a shoreline's wash of moon eclipsed by cloud.

A dream saved is this glass of water
which lights a piecemeal, bizarre version of a room,
encrypts and reverses a text in progress,
swells, presses flat, these fingertips.
As the day warms, the glass collects dust,
fresh shadows, kaleidoscopes gold air.
You sip from it, drinking the room, the dream:
here and now and then; nowhere, never.

Solstice

A night of broken sleep, spotlit islands
of recall adrift on a dark sea –
life-fragments passing by as if
in slow-motion anticipation of death.
At first light, again I wake –
though from hours' or minutes' sleep,

                  who could say?

The dream that claimed those last seconds
slips, tries to lose itself, holds fast:
a spirit level's eye of air

              brought to stillness.

At this pivot of the year, the bundled body
craves oblivion, the depthless downward;
yet craves, too, its deliverance –
the cycle of return bringing new fuel,
the breach of seed coats in the sod.

Room

My mind, like this room, fills with early light,
riffs of bird song. The lamp still on,
shadows crowd the walls: my vague form
propped against pillows; this hand, its looming pen
ready to track firefly glimmers, to record
with an engraver's care, truths
harsh or consoling.
     In this poem now
I seek refuge from a friend's anger
that has pressed its toxic freight into
breasts and tongue and heart:
     the places from which one gives.
I switch the lamp off, touch the cold
windowpane. Sparrows lift from the grass,
alight in a sheoak sparking in the wind.
A blackbird bathes on the rainy path.

Figure in a Room

on Vermeer's *Woman in Blue Reading a Letter*

Daylight falls most lavishly
on brow, on clasping hands, and the curve
made by her soon-to-be-born child.
Her form is sheathed in silken blue and brown:
chiaroscuro of earth and sky.
The map with its umber veins, its cambered
gleam, backgrounds her upper body:
portrait within a portrait.
                            Today's clouds
white-blue as the walls of her room,
slide over the glassed-in scene.
                            On her table,
a pearl necklace, the letter's first page. She reads on,
brushed by reflections of muslin curtains,
their ghostly sway framing trunk and branches,
birds joining points on a leafy map.

Portrait

on Vermeer's *Girl with a Pearl Earring*

The gold waterfall of her turban,
its lazuli bands, are brought into relief,
nuanced, by the sombre, subversive shades
lurking in folds, cupping chin and cheekbones,
and sculpting the richest garments one might wish for
to clothe human hope and sweet promise.

The chaste collar, the pearl's milky arc, accord with
the sheened whiteness of her hazel eyes;
in their depths – transparent, forever
unknown to us – I read of fears mastered.
She stands poised at the meeting points between
youth and fate, between flesh and eternity.
Her diamond self waits, her angled gaze tests
the contract between seeing and believing.

Morning

First light, or an efflorescence of darkness?
Doors glimmer between fact and dream,
gather substance; the bookcase fills with distinct
spines, each a claim on memory.
Across the housefront and lawn of Le Sidaner's
Table in the Sun, slabs of brightness;
buttery flecks on birch trunk, vined archways,
the blue tablecloth, the scarf-draped chair.

Above my lampshade's sea-green, Vuillard's
Woman Sewing before a Garden Window.
A golden glare the trellis cuts to diamonds
picks out the white on her chequered gown,
clasps nape, shoulders. Bowed over a shapeless
shape, she makes and mends, almost faceless.

At Winter's Turning

I reach the bus shelter before dawn.
The lowest star is spilt phosphorus,
the rest, studies in undying absence.
A mild wind touches my face, my cold hands.
At seven, a hyacinth mist fills
the glass wall of the pool, translates into
the swaying silver-mauve I swim towards.

After a day of writing, the journey home
under a sky crowded with gloomy thoughts
but allowing winged dreams, lanterns
of sunset pink.
                    The bus swings towards the sea.
Low clouds form a second line of hills
inset with gold leaf, then with ivory.
All colour gone, the sky's a glowing page.

After the Rain

Unlocking the door, I step into winter's
closed, infinite room, a pulled thread of grief
down my body's left side. An ashen glare
bears down from a sky of shovelled snow.
At the park, spatters of light soak my shoes;
I lean into hunched shoulders of wind.

Strung from taupe and cream paperbark
a web, minutely pearled. Its mesh holds
eucalypts, the oval busy with dogs.
Would that I might stumble upon a detour
into the heart of the matter – so I think
as I trudge on. This, it would seem,
is weather for visiting unreclaimed selves
crying with diamond beaks from a packed nest.

Early

The first sorties of black cormorants
pulse seaward through olive-gold.
I go forth to consult with my familiars:
A heron alights on an aerial, its form
altering as it preens and the wind stirs
head crest, strokes grey bustles, chestnut cravat;
eye and beak one dark line, it reads the heavens,
takes in the day, bird-watches.
Terns romp en masse above the river,
with inspired verve out-arguing the wind.
In gold-trimmed grey, a honeyeater
sets down on the green shipping beacon –
so keen of eye; wings, suavely at rest –
then swims over the town, its Atlantis.

The Long Fields, the Cliffs

A black-shouldered kite lifts from
makeshift stillness, is suddenly elsewhere,
poised on a shelf of air to lipread
the undergrowth's secret mouths – a flame
fed by desire but in love with distance.
It counters the wind's will, relentlessly
patient, centering on the unseen.

A shift like a stalled pounce, the governed
fall through sun blaze, the dark thorn of its beak
ready to swipe, twist through
a small piece of creation.
After, the rhythmic ascent until it hangs
cloud-white against a cloudless sky,
that rubied gaze, a burning-glass.

At the Cliffs

I'd hoped for a marsh harrier, keeping
its place in the wind – a bookmark between
airy pages – or some voyager from
Antarctica, in its white glide the carved
silence of ice. My gaze hovers, sweeps over
that crack in the sea: a fault-line of foam
jagged as a gull's flight through storm.

The rip tracks shoreward, past where surfers
skate and bounce along glass arcades,
skidding down as snowy paws clamber
towards the rock-shelf – beyond which the dunes,
fragile haunt of the red-cap, ascend through
marram reefs to these cliffs: laced with gale-blown
shell grit; algae; the bones of birds and fish.

Red-Capped Plover

Set within so much vastness
that one red-cap on the empty shore
stayed focal long after its quick flight
had defeated my eyes and it vanished
through a pinpoint high above the river,
marrying lightness with light.

Nearby, in nest-scrapes under the cliffs,
red-caps raise their young, ready to draw off
dogs or marauding birds by miming
a wounded wing. Although, in my field guide,
the map of Australia is dark with them,
in this place they're threatened. I imagine
dots of space appearing, spreading over
that blackness – *here*, then *there*, and *there...*

Hooded Plovers

At the 'Heritage Centre', sea creatures
in aerated tanks, and blank-eyed tableaux
of shearwaters, sandpipers, gulls.
I take a 'Save the Hoodie' leaflet,
ask about sightings, numbers. The latest news:
a fledging this very day... but the nest-scrape's
other chicks were lost – foxes, or humans?

On a lit screen, plovers on shining sand,
their quiet beauty archived.
I imagine new chicks, puff-balls of light,
running among the dunes.
                                   Hoping for no such joys,
that they're nested out of common view,
I make for the ocean, its merest swirl
swamping footprints, dragging them smooth.

Terns

who fly epic arcs, slipping through
atmospheres, past sleeping continents –
so good at bathing, too: cajoling brine
over wings with shivering leaps backwards
then a final shimmy ten feet above
as if to baptise their former selves.
Next, the charisma of flight – their bodies
such an ingenious fit with the world
as they side-swipe the wind, ride its back
to reconnoitre the river, make lightning-culls
from the hearts of sudden white flowers.
Later they stand, dumpy yet winsome
on mirror sand, facing out to sea:
their eyes calm, gleaming like homely stars.

Four Black-Winged Stilts

As if linked by elastic thread, they lift,
trail their weightless grace to the Spit –
botanical, somehow, with tapering
leaf-wings, and stem-legs. They forage then rise
as one again, drift serenely through
adverse winds towards their spot on the river,
touching down at the same instant.

Stilt hatchlings – fill-in-the-dots bodies,
sturdy legs half their height, fine bills a pointer
of things to come – are most easily found
in field guides, their toes planted on inky earth.
Their future is to frequent marshlands,
make slow forays across water –
sometimes, with soul mates in triplicate.

Crossing the Estuary

1.

A storm-sky has moved in
like one country over another.
Launches throb upstream through smoky strafes of rain:
a man pressed to a rail, scales a ten-pound snapper.
I wade in, nerved to cross
for the first time, this brimming gateway.

My arms cut black light, I sway forwards,
a cipher above the river's hidden life.
Old fears course through me – the real journey
so much longer than the one imagined.
Then I rise through my own weight, print sand
alive with scuttling shards of rainbow.
The first shore, its jetty and cypresses
flash white, the storm breaks.
                    Breath slowed, I stroll back in.

2.

Mid-river, a backwash of panic claims me.
I tread water, my neighbour a cormorant
superbly unfussed by my closeness,
the sheen of its eyes a meeting of noon and dusk,
its neck a beautiful question mark.
An utter presence; a closing mouth of water.

Once out in the humid air, I recall
the old warning about bodies of water,
lightning. My feet planted on drenched sand
I track the current until it falters,
slews sideways to where cataracts
tumble from grey horizons.
                              Shivering still,
I let the rain absolve me,
clothe my flesh in jubilance.

Birds at Dawn

I read through the small hours, tuned to white noise
as beyond the town, breakers peak, curl down:
we are both turning pages, the sea and I.
At first light a stroll through briny air
to where the deeps surge up towards flight.
A fulmar, a kelp gull, scan slopes
bursting with egret plumes.

Other birds manifest as collectives:
at the river, a profile of pelicans,
a sculpture park of herons;
above the waves, parabolas of swifts.
In dream light, dahlia-pink, my hand
lifts to block the gold centre of the flower;
I breathe the sea's breath, a mist of sound.

III

Old Age

You've reached the age of unexplained bruises:
mulberry stains on calf and forearm –
as if air itself could pressure such frail skin.
And what point now, in remembering
life's actual bumps and knocks? I massage
your swollen legs – or you do, preferring
the thick lavender creme, a second skin.

After days of deathly fatigue you walk outside –
the sun on your cheeks, an old friend;
keen eyes glean the garden's news, its tides
of renewal. Your raised hand points at
'The Happy Wanderer', profligate
on its trellis: 'See those red filaments?
That's where they'll appear, the new blooms.'

Spring Mornings

After the first hours, spent tuning poems,
I rise, gather the pages fallen to the floor
then start, methodically, to build the day.
The table set, I'll go to call you from sleep,
may find you like a wakeful child, waiting
to be saved from pain, or aloneness –
your breath laboured as a swimmer's in tall waves.
Rice cakes and jam, porridge, pills, tea.

In the garden, later, I'll massage your neck
while sunlight bathes your face, thin arms.
We'll take stock: violets, white and blue,
monbretias; soon, the irises.
All's well. Curved in on themselves,
mind, body, start to unfurl. *This freshness.*

These Days

'You're keeping me alive' – blunt words that hold
some truth. Veins embellish your temples;
your breath is shallow. The days unfold.
Even under my care, you'll sometimes wake
believing no one's here – you might be
on the moon. When I do leave, I write notes:
'Dear Mum, gone for a walk, back soon.'

On occasion, proud as a parent, I've found you –
feet up, music playing, biscuits and cheese –
your life going blithely on without me.
Some things – the day of the week, the recent past –
seem shadowy now. Summer draws near.
How you'll cope with its heat? How long can this go on?
I no longer worry. *The present moment.*

In Care

Not knowing what to do but go on
carrying the weight of another's life
as if it were my own. Two joined selves;
one starting, in body and mind, to die
then retrieving full life, to sit in this room
as if all were understood, and shared.

Slowly, you are not quite yourself:
the woman I know as gracious, lucidly
patient; a bearer and gifter of compassion.
Today, back from distance – from travelling
who knows where – your mantra of care:
'You do too much,' you diagnose,
innocent of the cure: ill health for me,
death for you; whichever knocks first.

Visits

In the taxi you ask, 'Where to, this time?'
My voice booms: 'The memory doctor first,
then the infection specialist.'
And tomorrow, your GP will clear your ears,
reduce your deafness – I won't have to shout
so loud across the widening ravine,
reach for my earplugs as your TV blares.

One day I'll wake to find the front door open,
rain belting in, filling an unknown footprint.
The world will change.
                              At the estuary,
waves chafed, faceted by the wind; hosts of ibis
pass through a sky taut with last light –
then the sound of coldness rushing
towards me, rushing away.

Hearts

The feeling invades my chest, tight, burdened.
There will be tests I won't tell you about.
I can imagine, but don't believe,
that this is grief in early instalments
or a tuning in to your worn-out heart
pounding towards the final lap.
Upright in your chair, you wait.

Who knows how long it takes to achieve peace:
living on, then, sustained by that peace,
so it can seem, remarkably,
that time is on your side.
                        Sequestered here
you track wattlebirds through sun-striped boughs –
the light in your eyes a friend to the day;
darkness, an old symbol, an accepted fact.

This Life

You rest a wall away. Often I hear
your softly staggered yawn, like small steps
into the day; even your silences.
And sometimes I'm called by a voice like yours
only to find you deep in sleep, breathing
as your mended, imperfect heart dictates.

We work at what will make the difference.
No need now to think of endings:
at this threshold, we think only of life –
feast on nectar and cakes, stroll the garden,
blessed by rain-cleansed air, magpies carolling.
Once we were as trees in drought, locked
from the source. Now, we replenish,
know peace, contemplate time's mercy.

Breath

Sleeplessness. At dawn, soft rain, the birds,
and music – Pachelbel's Canon played
over and over to soothe a mind still fazed
after a dizzy waking at one a.m. –
an alarm call to check on my mother.
With practised silence I opened her door,
in the quarter light leaned towards her face,
porcelain-pale, the strength of those fine bones,
to hear a breath. The same life-tide that swept us
apart has brought us to this grateful,
elegaic love, the hub we turn on –
Demeter and Kore becoming
each other, held in a graced affinity
between loss and loss. Twilight summer.

Before the Heat

In the dawn wind, letting it travel through
my body, transport me with freshened sight
to here. I pluck weeds, skirt the pumpkin vine
ramping out from the young apple tree.
A door slams. Inside, I find my mother
still beautifully asleep beneath
a coverlet of many greens patterned with
irises, waterlilies;
deep in her hip-bone, the infection
we live to outwit. The touch-lamp is on:
light answerable to fingertips.
All night, windows streamed with cool air.
Soon I'll shroud them ritually;
seal us inside this peace we have made.

Connections

I write few poems now, in thrall to your
perilous decline. Still prone to humour
you snipe, 'Next time, talk in English!'
after I've shouted to your deafness
down the phone, my hand cupped as if around
one of those jam-tins, linked by string,
known to us both in childhoods, worlds away.

You're present in the fit of my flesh;
no doubt you still can feel me at your body's core.
New life: a secret permeating its host,
getting ready to reveal... Who knows
what death is.
              Afterwards, you'll live
in the cells of memory, forever
hanging up that phone in amused disgust.

Respite Weekend

When I entered your room you'd cast off
the blankets, put the sheet over your face.
You were not dead, but wanted to be dead.
I lowered the sheet and kissed the white,
closed suffering of your face. It could make
no difference: you did not open your eyes...

I'd woken at six in a city hotel,
swum in the pool; then stood naked in my room,
writing the dream down lest it be
washed away by day's full light.

It can be almost time to die, one has
faced, accepted things – how one's life went,
present fear. But it's such hard work, Mother:
the waiting, the slow dying, the living on.

Parting
during my mother's last illness

If only we could all return
to each other – fulfil the great human dream
of belonging beyond death – the selves
we created, that were created through us,
reunited in some special nowhere.
Then we might explain our failure
to love enough, our sad
behaviour, what suffering did to us.

Will this sweet ease between us now,
find some way to persist after you're gone?
I console myself with the thought,
perhaps untrue, that each year
parted from you, I'll be drawing closer.
A friend's own answer: 'I choose to believe.'

Snapshot

All the world is green
            Tom Waits

2 p.m., mid-week, mid-spring.
We're in the green armchairs, looking out
at the hardenburgia – its sunstruck leaves
a shadow play on the flywire screen.
Through a rip, one leaf grows in towards us
wearing the light of this room, crosshatching
from the wire, the lilt of other leaf-tongues.

        Tom Waits is singing, wants everything
        to be fresh again; to forgive,
        be forgiven – while the world's clock grinds on,
        half-ironically, in the background.

Two quiet souls. Increasingly you love
this dusky stillness... Now you're off to bed.
I write the poem. The music ends.

Garden Portrait

my mother, side-view, under the moonah tree

There's a plainness to inner nobility,
a listening calm won from grief mastered.
So, in age, your profile portrait
comes into its own: pared down, refined,
telling a life through flesh and bone.
You sit, no viewer in sight,
looking at hazed light while looking within –
as into a tarn cupped by mountain
depths: lens to hawk, cloud, starburst.
What would I need to know, to wear sunlight
as richly, sparsely, as you do now:
your face tilted to receive the wind's balm;
that look of earthed serenity; body
poised as a cormorant's, wings outstretched.

Desert Flower

'The wheel must turn,' my father had said
when, stoic to the last, he lay dying.
And there it is again, rolling this way,
making ready to grind you down.

You believe, still, you can recover;
I nurse the hope you'll just slip away –
sleep the last, most dangerous refuge –
but not yet, not yet.
                          Your spirit has accomplished
the journey to the inner garden.
Your body's a desert flower – unbowed;
soon to be vanquished by sand-filled winds.
Amidst your afflictions, drops of kindness,
of sweet attention; your white-rimmed brown eyes
shine with a lifetime's love.

The Last Year

In answer to his words, the cliff opened its mouth – it yawned – it gaped.
Where there had been solid rock there was suddenly...

    'Ali Baba and the Forty Thieves'

They'd stopped by then, your half-filled crosswords
with their fey surmises – inspired leaps
from the backs of routine clues: 'a diving bird' –
awk, or *garnet*; 'biting insect' – *flee*...
keys not quite fitting, yet somehow turning
the lock. I glimpsed alcoves of dusty treasure:
kris – 'Malayan dagger'; *obi* –
'a Japanese sash'; *écus* – 'old French coins'.

You summoned bird names from the air –
rhea, erne – had the secrets of ponds and streams
at your fingertips: *eft*, *orfe* and *elver*,
were versatile: 'Twelve to Nero' – *X-I-I*;
solved in a trice the double clues:

'open', 'small seeds'; six letters.

                           You would have got that.

IV

.

Leaving

In my last days here, months after
you'd gone, there was an hour when,
sitting in your green armchair,
I felt myself so connected to that room,
my lungs to its air... my feet, heavy on the floor,
sensed the earth beneath, the tree roots, entangled,
held inside that close dark.

Every cell of my body had its story
of loss, of impacted fatigue, of desperation
as to how I might claim a future.
Every cell of my body felt the pull
that would have kept me here to walk through
these dim rooms, tend your garden.
And I got up, went to the window,
            looked out through the mirrored room.

A Life

In this tragic, miraculous world
one measure of our humanness is this –
the way we deal with affliction.

When, meeting its knife-shadow on the path,
we shape our answer, steadfastly
carry it through – each breath an act of courage –
we are brought closer to the mystery.

After the death of your infant son,
the gradual loss of all your siblings,
after twenty years a widow,
those last with chronic illness, you chose to say,
the night before you died, *I'm lucky.*

It's summer now. I pluck and hold an apricot
warm as a human face, against my cheek.

So it Goes

I brought you, long ago, great sorrow –
your clever, broken girl at pains to stand up
straight, get through the years of illness –
which somehow I survived, to become
a maker of poetry. But I'd claim as my best work
those six years spent with you in my care –
a small return for your undaunted love.

To receive life from the sweet-hearted
is a double gift. Yet mine was a childhood
without questions; beset by silences.
The stories I felt unable to voice
have gone into my bones. Perhaps they'll be shared
when we are both shadows inside the earth,
bones talking to bones; spirits in the trees.

Mother and Daughter

1.

I had just turned five. Dusty light
in the front room of our terrace house;
an empty hearth. I see again the nib pen,
a birthday gift from you, its glass stem
filled with shiny, lime-green water.

When I threw it against the iron grate
the locked-in, quicksilver bubbles – the bubbles
of my childhood rage – released into the air.

Again I hear your soft, heartbroken words:
'She doesn't love her Mummy.'
In that year, my infant brother had died.

The steel nib lay among slivers
in the cleaned grate: the air full of dust motes;
your grief, unanswered love; and my anger.

2.

The animus of early teenage years –
classic, written into the script:
hurts that stirred your rare anger.
Then you watched, without words or power
as I entered the tunnel I'd walk through for a decade.
Of what use was anger then, to either of us?

Your own years in the tunnel came later:
Bex powders and bingeing; and again,
no words. Trapped in annealed distance
I hardly knew of your despair.
But how could that be? You, so swift
to read whatever pain I felt –
the loving believer, the faithful one;
teacher of acceptance, lifelong.

3.

In mid-life before I learnt
how to answer your care.
      It's 1989,
the first year of your widowhood:
you've just undergone a triple bypass.
En route to the hospital, I stop
in St Kilda Road and ask myself
if I can do this – attend at this rebirth,
help to bring you back.

Then you are there before me –
sheathed in white, emerging still
from risky oblivion; but above the sheet
your thumb raised in the sign of hope, good luck,
your eyes, deeply clear
never for a moment doubting life, or me.

Hospital, 2004

1.

After your fall last year, I live with you now:
'Prevention's the name of the game.'
We share the cooking; I walk our dog.

When a new fall breaks your pelvis
I pack you in blankets, stroke your hair,
reassure until the ambulance comes.

The first operation botched; then another,
followed by complications. For many weeks
I spend each day at the hospital,
sit slouched in an armchair as we chew the fat,
your mind, as ever, razor-sharp;
both of us confined by this waiting
and freed by it, with time to work at the patience,
the belief, on which healing partly depends.

2.

'Who cares for the carer?' – the first question posed
on a training course taken long ago.
More than once, a watchful nurse stops me
to make that point. Right now, though,
I'm carrying your life; that's how it is.

A second nurse – dragon to her guardian angel –
eyes me blackly when, too tired to go out
and find a meal, I finish yours;
she'd rather the rubbish bin had that food.
My eyebrows lift, you wink, we are in cahoots.

You, Patricia, are my companion in this,
my guide, as I learn to give all –
you, whom I'll recognise at last,
after you've gone, as the love of my life.

3.

I watch over your progress, tend you,
take your part. Your beauty expert now,
I comb your hair, arrange for trims
and, with fingertips scented by
magic potions, give you facials inside
this small temple, the white bed-curtains drawn.

Before your return home, I buy jade-green
sheets, fat pillows. For the rest of your life –
it will be five years – a nurse will come
three times a week, to dress your hip wound.
You have a new bed; your room has been painted –
pink your colour of choice. All is arranged.
As you asked, I've bought chocolates
for the kindest nurses, flowers for them all.

Ritual

Of a friend's ill health, begun in youth,
you said: 'It was her life, you know.'
You did the Stations of the Cross with her
each Good Friday, completing the circuit
in the empty church. That final time –
you'd laugh about it after –
you guided her the wrong way round,
ending at the beginning of the Passion.

Always, you allowed for hope: each loss
a truth to be mourned in prayer, then lived beyond.
Years on, your friend would share, unknowingly,
the same hospital room. You stayed calm,
knew how to let things be; needed all your strength
to hold your nerve. To hope. To live beyond.

Death

In those last months, when you had slowed right down,
you'd still eat at the table, and sit outside
in the air of spring, then summer
but mostly you rested in your room. Small wounds
would not heal. 'I'm so tired,' you said –
and once, on a lapsing wave, your purchase on things
so tested, 'My poor old mind's all mangled.'

My hair was falling out. Fearing I'd break down,
that, in the small hours of some night
you'd need help I could not give,
I arranged a bed in care. Perhaps you thought
I was abandoning you. I couldn't explain.
Two days after Christmas, at what would later seem
the right time, you left us.

Eyewear

1.

I've kept – for well-intentioned years that stretched
to decades – the glasses that tracked our eyes' journeys.
I handle, first, the hard cases – a lacquered
red, and black, a coppery rose; squeeze
spring-mouthed sheaths of vinyl, grey or navy,
and this one, yours, a tapestried pouch.

Inside them, plastic frames – floridly
winged; squarely wide-eyed – too uncool
to rate as retro. The lenses rimmed with gold,
with titanium, slide out easily –
small, intellectual.
                                Will each pair find a match
when sent to Zambia, say, or Laos? –
someone ready to embrace a strange and bold
clarity, her gaze framed in a surprise.

2.

We looked at each other across rooms
in these relics – behind masking glazes
how many untold stories? And there were times
when it seemed I was known utterly –
that held gaze sustaining as
a hand pressed against the spine.

                                  We traversed
the last, shared years with pragmatic grace,
growing more, and less, short-sighted together.

Near the end, you left off wearing glasses,
believed you saw better without them.
Who was I to contest that? We watched
TV programmes, differently.
But the window birds stayed the same for you,
quick in the vine rooted beneath the house.

Travel Talk

at the Country Women's Association

1.

You asked for so little, I agreed:
a talk for your oldest friends – craftswomen;
makers of gingerbread, jam rolls, winged cupcakes;
sponsors of good works at home and abroad.
The topic: *Austria.* Though my visit there
had been years before, I felt jetlagged,
in a dead-meat tiredness. Fronting up
with notes desperately cribbed from *Go Europe*
I knew I'd found the right place: a poster of alps,
travel books heaped high; and, dangling from a hook
behind where I would stand, some lederhosen.
I so wanted not to disappoint,
tried to translate myself, bumbled through
like Joseph Cotton in *The Third Man.*

2.

At question time, someone asked if
the streets had been full of water. I took a detour,
punted us all down gold canals shimmering
with cupolas, pink-marble facades.
The spread was, but of course, revelatory.
There were Danish pastries – scenes from Aarhus
sped past my eyes – and scones, still warm,
crowned with glorious jam and glorious cream.
(I'd often travelled through Devonshire.)
That whipped cream, and the meringue above
lemon heaven, shone like snow on alps
as, to avoid small talk, I ate furiously,
believing I could hear – like some phantom
echo within my mind – the sound of music.

Luck

My mother threw pinches of spilt salt
over her left shoulder, would toss water
that had boiled eggs onto the garden;
crossed knives were swiftly uncrossed on the table.
For good luck: her youngest brother's signet ring,
its horseshoe worn smooth; the rabbit's foot
that was her mother's; a shamrock, four-leaved,
pressed inside her unused missal.

By small margins, sometimes, we find our way
or lose it. If charms that kiss the hem
of a frowning god, can help, let's have them.
Secure all mirrors, slip on the horseshoe ring
and then, with a pinch of salt, plant seeds where
the egg-water fell. Tend what grows there.

Games of Chance

remembering my mother and father

I watch as swathes of the human world become
more grasping, more seedily corrupt:
new cruelties spawned by cant, by despair,
by the pleasures of excess; the wantonly rich
and the power-mad still deep in love with war.

What price, then, the wise equanimity
with which you both met life, a shared composure
ritually set aside for those duels,
months-long, over scrabble and cribbage:
the ribbings, the loving insults, while scores went tipsy
yet balanced out, as if some peacemaker
were at the helm. Then once more, new volleys of
sparks from wit's tinderbox until one triumphed –
the other, poker-faced, biding their time.

Four Photographs

Here you are: in fox-fur cape with daphne spray;
dark eyes, dark hair; a warmly delicate smile:
fresh-lipped, trusting, your Irish mother's daughter.
And here she is, formal in black, vibrant,
knowing what she knows.
                                            As a girl you'd nursed her
through bouts of dengue, contracted in India.
Once, taking your hand, she had said:
'I've always thanked God for giving me you.'
Hours later, unexpectedly, her heart would fail.

Under the spinning fan, the frame around
you and my father, in middle age,
glimmers like light on water.
                                            In a small oval
the faces of two half-strangers who became as sisters,
able, at last, to guess the unsaid.

Journey

Light enters the sepia room.
Too late to clutch back sleep, blot out
a flight over three continents in one day,
four touchdowns; my ankles still swollen.
Here, a real summer after that spell of heat
abroad: a torched autumn before the snowlight.

At midnight, I'd thrown bags on the gravel
as you walked out – your nightdress and pale hair
framed by the lit house – to put your cheek on mine,
your arms around me as in my life's first hours...
but now, the embrace of friends versed in
give and take. Dawn birds are outsinging
a Bach cantata on the radio;
the room, a crystal steeped in honey.

Anniversary

at my mother's grave

Close overhead then climbing through
vicissitudes of air, the heron turns now
towards a silent ocean cupped between pines.
That was one prayer. This, another:
May you be at peace.
                    And may I,
carrying your memory with me,
find my wings' full power – moving through
troughs or crosswinds like the heron:
resilience and grace lifting it
from each new faltering.
                    And sometimes, dancing:
wings flowing into, out of themselves –
waves on a fantastical sea; the clasp and release
of nothingness – with, all the while, the slow ease
that will deliver it to nest, to silvered mudflat.

Heatwave

at Clifton Springs

Near dawn, my house still sweltering,
I walk up and down the driveway, breathing
slowly as rain comes, almost too soft to feel.
When it stops, the air is taut with new heat.
From the drive I can see the bay's dream-silver,
coral cinders in the east.

I'm remembering how, as I grew up
the moral rubric was to know your place,
not get above or ahead of yourself,
and later, too late, never to be down on yourself.
What, then? Walking past the plants in my nightdress,
buoyed by tinctured green fragrances
I wait for an edge of coolness: at home now
in this calm aloneness; this wakefulness.

Now

On the cliff path, early, the wind a cool shadow
felt at my back: when the sun's blaze slams
into my chest, I am held between them
as if both would claim me, pass though me.

So grief, with its heart-heat, its pressuring shadows,
lays claim, passes into and through us.
After, a stillness in which you may learn
from memories, know those who've gone
in new ways; and even imagine
their own past knowing of you.

My most frequent memory now
is of sitting in a room with them,

                                    my mother and father,
the sense of space and warmth in their presence
as, through the open house, air streams from the garden.

Walking

for my mother and father

Often I'll pace in the driveway, early –
twenty-five steps between the front gate
and the gate to the back garden where
a robinia harbours among its curled leaves
the first radiance, not yet a colour;
glints of pomegranate-red – or mauves, pinks,
the sky in a geranium mood.

Each instant of light is offered to us,
a boundless harvest until death.
To honour the light is to honour those
who brought us into it.
                              I remember
how they'd walk together through satined air,
their wordless genial pleasure
the cherishing of those who know the gift.

Five Years On

In Ireland last year I parted with
my particular grief, came back absolved;
no longer bereft, beholden.
But remembrance pulses on.
Whole cultures have been built on it,
have made of it a sacred observance,
and an art – the discerning of what the dead
ask of us, and how they feed our lives,
still, with glimmerings of wisdom.

The voices within us – some planted long ago
by them – have their conversations, suggest
how we might live now: more bravely,
more gracefully; tell us it is a marvellous thing
to stand simply in the light, accepting it.

Light and Water

Out watering the garden, the summer sun
still low, I watch the dusk inside a laurel
fill with spray – a glittering surge
                              speared by leaf shadows:
so intimate a transformation...
and here, reaching towards each plant,
the soft channels of sunlight shot through with
a billowing swirl I can change at will –
a rainstorm in miniature.

At noon, fishing boats on the ruffled bay –
their wakes now smooth, sky-bearing paths
that lead the gaze towards the mountains.
Under a cupola of gold glass
swallows write their silent, sacred music;
so much light and water known by those bright eyes.

The You Yangs

On clear days, indisputably there:
within the rain shadow of higher mountains,
that family of granite mounds –
a place gripped by the fertility of dryness,
where trees grow sideways from split rocks.
In winter, cloud-pools on boulders;
year-long, the deepened hollows conserve,
each cool gleam reflecting the life of shadows.

Today the mountains are a shaped absence
beyond the bay, a wall of haze sealed by
wave-spill curves. Always, an image of the bedrock;
a locus of vision, indigo on umber.
I climb towards dark light; kneeling
I cup my hands, drink from unseen wells.

In the You Yangs, the Yawangi Balug, a family group within the Wauthaurong
Aboriginal clan, enlarged hollows in and between rocks – first using fire to create
cracks, then working the stone – to form wells for the dry seasons.

The Bay

I'm old enough to have wondered
what my last memories will be,
young enough to seek out new ones that might,
in extremis, keep me company.

On a century-old pier stump, far out,
a cormorant airs its wings – a cross-shape against
the mountains, their violet darkness shared
in this light, by reefs in the shallow bay.

Where I wade, gold lines web the seabed,
trace each crinkling green surge. Even cloud-wreathed
the sun lays down a path towards me;
                                        the dolphins
pass unseen through that ribbed glitter, speed on,
their bronze-grey arcs threading the far stillness;
the peace of evening already present.

V

Visitor

Day after day bathers stand waist-deep
in cloudy gold, hoping to be chosen
by the dolphin, a scar down his left side,
who has come to live in the summer river.

On a cold shore, the waters sleek with sunrise,
a woman calls to him through the wind.
She tells me of their swim together –
weeks ago, before her stay in hospital.

In recovery still, she relives
the glide and surge of it, her fearlessness,
his pace mirroring her own;
and that one glimpse of his heedful eye.

It's said the dolphin remembers
those he partners: my first swim with him
a joyous, uncertain epic;
in the second, a brief ushering seaward.

Naturally, he favours strong swimmers, the young.
A girl, lithe and plucky,
arcs round him now, as he around her:
one entity, they plunge and spiral

for ecstatic minutes
that always will be with her – this dance amidst
sea-green veils and coursing sunlight
pearled by air, by eyes.

Barwon Heads, 2009

Acknowledgements

My thanks to the following publications in which many of these poems appeared. The Australian journals and newspapers: *The Age, The Australian, Australian Poetry Journal, Blast, Blue Dog, The Canberra Times, Meanjin, Southerly, The Sydney Morning Herald, Westerly*; in Ireland: *The Moth, Poetry Ireland Review, The SHOp, Southword, Skylight, The Yellow Nib*; in the U.K., *The Poetry Review*; in the U.S., *Antipodes*. The online journals: *Axon, Communion, Cordite, Divan, Eureka Street, Mascara, Plumwood Mountain, Tinteán* and *Zeitschrift für Australienstudien, issue 24, 2010*. The anthologies: *The Best Australian Poetry 2005*, ed. Peter Porter (Brisbane: UQP, 2005); *The Best Australian Poems 2011*, ed. John Tranter (Melbourne: Black Inc., 2011); *The Best Australian Poems 2012*, ed. John Tranter (Melbourne: Black Inc., 2012); *The Best Australian Poems 2013*, ed. Lisa Gorton (Melbourne: Black Inc., 2013); *The Best Australian Poems 2014*, ed. Geoff Page (Melbourne: Black Inc., 2014); *Eclogues: Newcastle Poetry Prize Anthology 2007; The Wombat Vedas: Newcastle Poetry Prize Anthology 2011; Once Wild: Newcastle Poetry Prize Anthology 2014; Australian Poetry Anthology 2014*, ed. Lucy Dougan & Martin Langford; *Australian Poetry Anthology 2015*, ed. Sarah Holland-Batt & Brook Emery; *Australian Love Poems 2013*, ed. Mark Tredinnick (Melbourne: Inkerman & Blunt, 2013); *Notes for the Translators*, ed. Christopher Kelen (ASM, Macao 2013); *The turnrow Anthology of Contemporary Australian Poetry*, ed. John Kinsella (Louisiana: turnrow Books, 2014); *Pedagogy and Edusemiotics: Theoretical Challenges/Practical Opportunities*, ed. Inna Semetsky and Andrew Stables (Rotterdam: Sense Publishers, 2014).

'Feeding the Birds', 'Before the Heat', 'Breath', 'At the Cliffs' and 'Terns' also appear in Diane Fahey's *The Wing Collection: New & Selected Poems* (Puncher & Wattmann: Sydney, 2011).

A number of poems appear in revised versions, some with changed titles.

The haiku quoted in 'Spring' is from *Love and Barley – Haiku of Basho*, translated by Lucien Stryk.

My warmest gratitude to my friends Rosemary Blake, Sandy Fitts, Katherine Gallagher and Miriel Lenore for their comments on various poems.

And to Helen Byrne, RN, my heartfelt thanks for her care of my mother.

About the Author

Diane Fahey was born in Melbourne and now lives in a bayside town on the Bellarine Peninsula in Victoria. She is the author of twelve poetry collections, most recently *The Wing Collection: New & Selected Poems* and *The Stone Garden: Poems from Clare*, both shortlisted for major book awards. *Sea Wall and River Light*, a collection of poems set in Barwon Heads, received the ACT government's Judith Wright Poetry Award in 2007. Among her awards for individual poems are the Newcastle Poetry Prize and the Wesley Michel Wright Award. Diane has received literary grants from the Victorian and South Australian Governments, and from the Australia Council, including a grant in 2014 to support the writing of a book on the West of Ireland. She took part in Australian Poetry's 2013 International Poetry Tour of Ireland. Past writing residencies have taken her to Venice, the Tyrone Guthrie Centre in Ireland, Hawthornden Castle International Writers' Retreat in Scotland, and to Varuna, the National Writers House, and Bundanon, both in N.S.W. She has been writer in residence at Ormond College, Melbourne, and the University of Adelaide. In 2000, Diane Fahey was awarded a PhD in Creative Writing from the University of Western Sydney for her study, 'Places and Spaces of the Writing Life'. Her website: dianefaheypoet.com

www.ingramcontent.com/pod-product-compliance
Lightning Source LLC
Chambersburg PA
CBHW030957090426
42737CB00007B/575